1

WOULD YOU RATHER HOLD A BOA CONSTRICTOR OR HOLD A TARANTULA FOR ONE HOUR?

2

WOULD YOU RATHER BURP IN FRONT OF YOUR TEACHER OR FART LOUDLY IN A LIBRARY?

3

WOULD YOU RATHER SMELL YOUR FRIEND'S BREATH OR HAVE A FRIEND SMELL YOUR OWN BREATH?

4

WOULD YOU RATHER PLAY IN A MUD PIT FILLED WITH WORMS AND SLUGS OR PLAY IN A BATH OF ROTTING FISH?

5

WOULD YOU RATHER HAVE CHEWING GUM STUCK IN YOUR HAIR OR YOUR NOSTRILS FILLED WITH TOOTHPASTE?

Over 350 hilarious gross & crazy
Would You Rather Questions
4 Everyone!

(These are questions are for you
to ask. DO NOT attempt any of
these questions. We are not
responsible for your actions.)

Don't forget the BONUS
questions at the end of the book!

6

WOULD YOU RATHER HAVE SOMEONE SNEEZE ON YOUR FACE OR HAVE SOMEONE FART IN YOUR FACE?

7

WOULD YOU RATHER DUNK YOUR HEAD IN A BUCKET OF KETCHUP OR A POOL OF CHILI?

8

WOULD YOU RATHER DRINK A GALLON OF PICKLE JUICE OR A GALLON OF TOMATO JUICE?

9

WOULD YOU RATHER WATCH A TWO-HOUR MOVIE OF SOMEONE SQUEEZING BLACKHEADS OR PICK YOUR PARENTS' NOSE?

10

WOULD YOU RATHER LICK CHEWING GUM OFF THE GROUND OR LICK THE SIDEWALK IN FRONT OF A CROWD OF PEOPLE?

11

WOULD YOU RATHER WALK AROUND THE CITY IN ONLY YOUR UNDERWEAR OR WALK AROUND THE CITY WITH UNDERWEAR ON YOUR HEAD SINGING LOUDLY AT THE TOP OF YOUR LUNGS?

12

WOULD YOU RATHER GET CHASED BY AN ARMY OF ENORMOUS COCKROACHES OR AN ARMY OF JUMPING SPIDERS?

13

WOULD YOU RATHER GET AN F ON YOUR HOMEWORK OR EAT YOUR HOMEWORK?

14

WOULD YOU RATHER BE TRAPPED IN A TRUCK STOP BATHROOM OR THE CITY DUMP FOR 1 DAY?

15

WOULD YOU RATHER BE THROWN UP ON BY YOUR FRIEND OR PEED ON BY YOUR FRIEND?

16

WOULD YOU RATHER CLEAN SOMEONE ELSE'S EARS OR CLIP THEIR TOENAILS?

17

WOULD YOU RATHER BURP OR FART 30 TIMES A DAY FOR THE REST OF YOUR LIFE?

18

WOULD YOU RATHER BE COVERED IN PEANUT BUTTER OR COVERED IN JELLY?

19

WOULD YOU RATHER HAVE A FART GUN OR A STINK BOMB TO DEFEND YOURSELF AGAINST AN ARMY OF RABID SQUIRRELS?

20

WOULD YOU RATHER PICK LINT OUT OF YOUR FRIEND'S BELLY BUTTON OR PICK EAR WAX OUT OF YOUR FRIEND'S EARS?

21
WOULD YOU RATHER DRINK A GLASS OF SWEAT OR STICK YOUR HAND IN A JAR OF SNOT?

22
WOULD YOU RATHER HAVE SARDINES OR RAW EGGS BE THROWN AT YOU EVERY TIME YOU LEFT YOUR HOUSE?

23
WOULD YOU RATHER BE TRAPPED IN A SMALL ROOM FULL OF TARANTULAS FOR 3 HOURS OR HAVE TO SLEEP IN A BED FILLED WITH WORMS?

24
WOULD YOU RATHER UNCONTROLLABLY SWEAT ALL DAY OR SMELL LIKE TUNA FISH ALL DAY?

25
WOULD YOU RATHER LIVE IN A WORLD COVERED ENTIRELY IN GREEN SNOT OR COVERED ENTIRELY IN COW MANURE?

26

WOULD YOU RATHER HAVE A COLLECTION OF ARMPIT HAIR OR COLLECTION OF FINGERNAIL CLIPPINGS?

27

WOULD YOU RATHER HAVE THE BOOGER MONSTER TAKE OVER THE CITY OR THE FART MONSTER TAKE OVER THE CITY?

28

WOULD YOU RATHER DRINK A GLASS OF WATER FROM A PIG TROUGH OR DRINK A GLASS OF RUSTY WATER THAT HAS BEEN SITTING FOR 2 MONTHS?

29

WOULD YOU RATHER HAVE FEET THAT ITCHED ALL DAY LONG OR SMELLY FEET THAT MADE PEOPLE RUN AWAY?

30

WOULD YOU RATHER COUGH OUT MUCUS EVERY TIME YOU OPENED YOUR EYES OR HAVE SNOT SPONTANEOUSLY SHOOT OUT THROUGH YOUR NOSE WHENEVER SOMEONE SAID HI TO YOU?

31

WOULD YOU RATHER HAVE A FRIEND FART ON YOUR FACE OR A DOG FART ON YOUR FACE?

32

WOULD YOU RATHER HAVE A LARGE STOMACH THAT ALWAYS GROWLED REALLY LOUDLY LIKE A BEAR OR A BIG NOSE THAT BUZZED WHEN YOU TALKED?

33

WOULD YOU RATHER NOT BE ABLE TO WASH YOUR HANDS FOR ONE MONTH OR NOT BE ABLE TO WASH YOUR HAIR FOR ONE MONTH?

34

WOULD YOU RATHER HAVE A BIRD POOP ON YOUR HEAD OR USE YOUR SLEEVE AS TISSUE AND BLOW YOUR NOSE?

35

WOULD YOU RATHER SWIM IN A DIRTY POOL WITH A PIG OR PLAY IN A PILE OF GARBAGE?

36
WOULD YOU RATHER BE SMACKED IN THE FACE BY ROADKILL OR COOK IT UP FOR DINNER?

37
WOULD YOU RATHER LICK SAND OR LICK HOT WAX?

38
WOULD YOU RATHER EAT A BOWL OF MAYONNAISE OR A BOWL OF MUSTARD?

39
WOULD YOU RATHER BE STRANDED ON A DESERT ISLAND WITH A SHOVEL OR A BAG OF APPLES?

40
WOULD YOU RATHER WASH DISHES WITH TOILET WATER FOR ONE WEEK OR USE THE KITCHEN SINK AS A TOILET FOR ONE WEEK?

41

WOULD YOU RATHER WEAR CLOTHES WITH DOG HAIR ALL OVER IT OR FIND HUMAN HAIR IN YOUR FOOD?

42

WOULD YOU RATHER WEAR SHOES TWO SIZES TOO SMALL OR HAVE DOG POOP ON THE BOTTOM OF YOUR SHOE?

43

WOULD YOU RATHER LICK SOMEONE'S DIRTY ARMPIT OR IN BETWEEN THEIR DIRTY TOES?

44

WOULD YOU RATHER LICK SOMEONE'S SWEATY ARMPIT OR EAT A STRAND OF SOMEONE'S GREASY HAIR?

45

WOULD YOU RATHER EAT ANCHOVY-FLAVORED CHIPS OR PICKLE-FLAVORED CANDY?

46

WOULD YOU RATHER NEVER SHOWER AGAIN OR NEVER BRUSH YOUR TEETH AGAIN?

47

WOULD YOU RATHER LICK THE BOTTOM OF AN OUTHOUSE OR EAT YOUR BOOGERS FOR LUNCH?

48

WOULD YOU RATHER BE A SNAIL OR A RAT FOR THE REST OF YOUR LIFE?

49

WOULD YOU RATHER HAVE NOODLES FOR HAIR OR CANDY CORN FOR TEETH?

50

WOULD YOU RATHER EAT WASABI PIZZA OR TARTAR SAUCE BROWNIES?

51
WOULD YOU RATHER SMELL SOMEONE ELSE'S ROTTEN TOOTH BREATH OR YOUR DOG'S POOP?

52
WOULD YOU RATHER WEAR SMELLY SHOES FOR A YEAR OR HAVE TO GO BAREFOOT FOR A YEAR?

53
WOULD YOU RATHER CHEW SOMEONE ELSE'S BUBBLE GUM OR EAT A WHOLE JAR OF PICKLED SAUERKRAUT?

54
WOULD YOU RATHER SPIT OUT A FUR BALL LIKE A CAT OR FART OUT RAINBOWS LIKE A UNICORN?

55
WOULD YOU RATHER HAVE THE ABILITY TO TRANSFORM INTO A COCKROACH OR TRANSFORM INTO A RAT?

56

WOULD YOU RATHER BE A GOAT OR NEVER GO ANYWHERE AGAIN WITHOUT BEING CHASED BY A GOAT?

57

WOULD YOU RATHER GO OUT WEARING INVISIBLE CLOTHES OR SEE YOUR GRANDMA NAKED?

58

WOULD YOU RATHER BE CHASED BY A CLOWN OR A GIANT COCKROACH?

59

WOULD YOU RATHER HAVE THE ABILITY TO PUKE OUT FLOWERS OR HAVE FARTS THAT SMELL LIKE FLOWERS?

60

WOULD YOU RATHER WEAR A TOILET PLUNGER AS A HAT OR DIRTY UNDERWEAR AS A HAT?

61
WOULD YOU RATHER HAVE PHLEGM IN YOUR HAIR OR IN YOUR HAND?

62
WOULD YOU RATHER GO TO SCHOOL SMELLING LIKE ROTTEN FISH OR STINKY CHEESE?

63
WOULD YOU RATHER SIT IN A PUDDLE OF GROUND UP ANCHOVIES FOR 1 HOUR OR SIT IN A PUDDLE OF COW MANURE FOR 1 HOUR?

64
WOULD YOU RATHER EAT CHICKEN FEET OR PIG FEET FOR DINNER?

65
WOULD YOU RATHER HAVE A FOOD FIGHT IN A SCHOOL CAFETERIA WITH YOUR PRINCIPAL WATCHING OR FOOD FIGHT AT A FINE-DINING RESTAURANT?

66
WOULD YOU RATHER HAVE TO EAT A CAN OF SARDINES FOR SCHOOL LUNCH OR SKIP LUNCH?

67
WOULD YOU RATHER SCRAPE GUM UNDER THE TABLE AND EAT IT OR CLEAN A TOILET BOWL AND DRINK IT?

68
WOULD YOU RATHER EAT A BOWL OF WORM SOUP OR HAVE A HUNDRED SPIDERS CRAWL UP YOUR ARM?

69
WOULD YOU RATHER HAVE A HUGE, PERMANENT WART ON YOUR FOREHEAD OR HAVE COARSE NOSE HAIR THAT GROWS 1 INCH EVERY HOUR?

70
WOULD YOU RATHER SPONTANEOUSLY SNEEZE ON THE HOUR FOR AN ENTIRE DAY OR SNEEZE ALL OVER YOUR TEACHER'S FACE?

71

WOULD YOU RATHER EAT ICE CREAM OFF THE DIRTY GROUND OR EAT LEFTOVER CHICKEN LIVER?

72

WOULD YOU RATHER HIDE IN A TRASHCAN OR IN AN OUTHOUSE?

73

WOULD YOU RATHER USE HOT SAUCE AS EYE DROPS OR DRINK A BOTTLE OF VINEGAR?

74

WOULD YOU RATHER HAVE CLOTHES MADE OUT OF CAT HAIR OR CLOTHES MADE OUT OF PIG SKIN?

75

WOULD YOU RATHER HAVE THE ABILITY TO SEE A MILE AWAY OR HEAR EVERYTHING THAT ANYBODY SAYS FOR A MILE AWAY?

76

WOULD YOU RATHER BE IN A REAL LIFE HORROR MOVIE OR LOOK LIKE A CREEPY CLOWN?

77

WOULD YOU RATHER COUGH INCESSANTLY FOR ONE HOUR OR SNEEZE SO LOUD THAT YOUR EARS RING FOR AN HOUR?

78

WOULD YOU RATHER BE INVISIBLE AND GORGEOUS OR VISIBLE AND UGLY?

79

WOULD YOU RATHER CLEAN OUT AN OUTHOUSE OR CLEAN OUT A PIG STY?

80

WOULD YOU RATHER RECEIVE A WET WILLY OR A WEDGIE ONCE PER DAY?

81

WOULD YOU RATHER GO DUMPSTER DIVING OR WADE SHOULDER-DEEP INTO A MUD PIT?

82

WOULD YOU RATHER STOP CUTTING YOUR TOENAILS OR STOP SHOWERING FOR ONE MONTH?

83

WOULD YOU RATHER HAVE THE ABILITY TO SEE EVERYTHING—AND THINGS YOU WISH YOU COULDN'T SEE—OR HAVE THE ABILITY TO HEAR AND UNDERSTAND EVERYTHING?

84

WOULD YOU RATHER SNIFF A MONKEY'S FEET OR LICK A GOAT'S BEARD?

85

WOULD YOU RATHER STICK YOUR HAND IN A BUCKET OF WORMS OR A BUCKET OF ANTS?

86

WOULD YOU RATHER HAVE REALLY LONG LEGS AND SUPER SHORT ARMS, OR SUPER SHORT LEGS AND REALLY LONG ARMS?

87

WOULD YOU RATHER BE A RAT OR A GIANT WORM?

88

WOULD YOU RATHER TAKE A SHOWER WITH A TOILET SCRUBBER OR USE YOUR OWN SHIRT AS TOILET PAPER?

89

WOULD YOU RATHER WASH YOUR HANDS WITH A SPIKY PORCUPINE OR WASH YOUR HAIR WITH A SPONGE MADE FROM SKUNK SKIN?

90

WOULD YOU RATHER EAT A HALF-EATEN CHEESEBURGER OUT OF THE TRASH OR FIND A WORM IN YOUR CHICKEN NUGGET?

91

WOULD YOU RATHER HAVE FLEAS LIKE A DOG OR COUGH OUT FUR BALLS LIKE A CAT?

92

WOULD YOU RATHER ENTER A HOT DOG EATING CONTEST OR A SKY DIVING CONTEST?

93

WOULD YOU RATHER HAVE A BLACK, FORKED TONGUE OR HAVE YOUR BREATH SMELL LIKE ROTTEN MEAT FOR THE REST OF YOUR LIFE?

94

WOULD YOU RATHER BRUSH YOUR TEETH WITH ROTTEN-EGG TOOTHPASTE OR EAT FISH-FLAVORED ICE CREAM?

95

WOULD YOU RATHER LOSE YOUR KEYS IN A TUB FULL OF MELTED NACHO CHEESE OR HAVE TO EAT A WHOLE GALLON OF NACHO CHEESE?

96

WOULD YOU RATHER HAVE TO PUT ON A BEAR SUIT AND DANCE IN 100 DEGREE HEAT FOR 30 MINUTES OR BE THROWN INTO AN ICE POND?

97

WOULD YOU RATHER SWEAT ORANGE JUICE OR HAVE APPLE JUICE TEARS?

98

WOULD YOU RATHER HAVE THE BODY OF A FLY OR THE HEAD OF A FLY?

99

WOULD YOU RATHER EAT FLIES LIKE A TOAD OR EAT FLEAS LIKE A MONKEY?

100

WOULD YOU RATHER HAVE A BOXING MATCH WITH AN OSTRICH OR HAVE YOUR COMPETITIVE DANCE PARTNER BE A GORILLA?

101

WOULD YOU RATHER HAVE EYE LASHES MADE FROM INSECT LEGS OR LIPS FROM A PIG SNOUT?

102

WOULD YOU RATHER BE THE MOST POPULAR KID IN SCHOOL AND HAVE TERRIBLE GRADES, OR BE A LONER WITH STRAIGHT A'S?

103

WOULD YOU RATHER HAVE THE POWER TO CONTROL MOSQUITOS OR THE POWER TO CONTROL BEES?

104

WOULD YOU RATHER USE YOUR FRIEND'S TOOTHBRUSH OR SHAVE YOUR FRIEND'S ARMPITS?

105

WOULD YOU RATHER EAT BAT PASTE OR A WHOLE SHEEP'S HEAD?

106

WOULD YOU RATHER EAT PANCAKES WITH MUSTARD OR EAT A HOT DOG WITH FROSTING?

107

WOULD YOU RATHER HAVE THE POWER TO CONTROL THE WEATHER OR THE POWER TO CONTROL TIME?

108

WOULD YOU RATHER YOUR MOUTH RESEMBLE A DONKEY OR YOUR NOSE RESEMBLE A PIG?

109

WOULD YOU RATHER HAVE A PURSE MADE OUT OF PIG INTESTINES OR A WALLET MADE FROM FISH EYES?

110

WOULD YOU RATHER WALK BAREFOOT FOR 5 MILES ON A SIDEWALK COVERED IN WORMS OR EAT A GRASSHOPPER TACO?

111

WOULD YOU RATHER GET LICKED BY A PIG OR GET KISSED BY A MONKEY?

112

WOULD YOU RATHER GET HIT BY BIRD POOP OR SNEEZED IN THE FACE BY A HORSE?

113

WOULD YOU RATHER PUKE WORMS OR SNEEZE ANTS?

114

WOULD YOU RATHER SLEEP WITH A PILLOW MADE OF RAW BACON OR HAVE A BLANKET MADE FROM A BEE HIVE?

115

WOULD YOU RATHER LIVE IN A HOUSE MADE OUT OF MAGGOTS OR EAT A MAGGOT-FILLED BURRITO?

116

WOULD YOU RATHER HAVE YOUR FACE ON YOUR BUTT OR YOUR BUTT ON YOUR FACE?

117

WOULD YOU RATHER HAVE THE POWER TO FART OR BURP ON COMMAND?

118

WOULD YOU RATHER KISS SOMEONE WITH COLD SORES ALL OVER THEIR LIPS OR KISS A FROG?

119

WOULD YOU RATHER BE A VOMIT COLLECTOR OR A WORK IN A MORGUE?

120

WOULD YOU RATHER BE BORN WITH LIZARD SKIN OR BAT WINGS?

121

WOULD YOU RATHER COOK DINNER INSIDE AN OUTHOUSE OR EAT A COCKROACH?

122

WOULD YOU RATHER YOUR COOKING MAKE EVERYONE SICK AT THANKSGIVING DINNER OR VOMIT ALL OVER YOUR FAMILY'S CHRISTMAS DINNER?

123

WOULD YOU RATHER IT RAIN GRAVY OR HAVE A SNOWBALL FIGHT WITH MASHED POTATOES?

124

WOULD YOU RATHER SLEEP NEXT TO A KOALA BEAR OR SHAVE A MONKEY'S BACK?

125

WOULD YOU RATHER CHEW GUM THAT TASTES LIKE PICKLES OR BRUSH YOUR TEETH WITH HOT SAUCE?

126

WOULD YOU RATHER HAVE YOUR BODY BE COVERED WITH FUR OR HAVE EVERY HAIR ON YOUR BODY PLUCKED OFF FOREVER?

127

WOULD YOU RATHER DRINK WATER OUT OF A FISH TANK OR EAT THE FISH?

128

WOULD YOU RATHER YOUR BEST FRIEND TURN INTO A WEREWOLF OR BE A HOSTAGE IN A BANK ROBBERY?

129

WOULD YOU RATHER HAVE UNDERWEAR MADE FROM SOGGY BREAD OR SANDPAPER?

130

WOULD YOU RATHER MAKE A GOURMET MEAL USING YOUR TOENAILS OR YOUR SNOT?

131
WOULD YOU RATHER HAVE GLOWING GREEN EYES OR A FORKED TONGUE?

132
WOULD YOU RATHER CUT OFF ANOTHER PERSON'S FOOT CALLUS OR POP THEIR ZITS?

133
WOULD YOU RATHER EAT A LIVE SQUID SANDWICH EVERYDAY FOR LUNCH FOR THE REST OF YOUR LIFE OR GET YOUR PINKY BIT OFF BY A SHARK?

134
WOULD YOU RATHER EAT CHOCOLATE PUDDING THAT TASTES LIKE COCKROACH OR A COCKROACH THAT TASTE LIKE CHOCOLATE PUDDING?

135
WOULD YOU RATHER SPEND THE NIGHT IN A SEWER OR DIG IN A DUMPSTER AND FIND A DEAD BODY?

136

WOULD YOU RATHER EAT THE HAIR FROM A SHOWER DRAIN OR LOSE YOUR FRONT TOOTH PERMANENTLY?

137

WOULD YOU RATHER CLOG A TOILET EVERY TIME YOU USED IT OR HAVE UNCONTROLLABLE DIARRHEA?

138

WOULD YOU RATHER SMELL LIKE ROTTEN EGGS OR LOSE YOUR ABILITY TO TALK?

139

WOULD YOU RATHER GET IN A FIGHT WITH SPIT WADS OR WITH FART BOMBS?

140

WOULD YOU RATHER EAT A SANDWICH COVERED IN FRUIT FLIES OR EAT SAUTEED FROG LEGS?

141
WOULD YOU RATHER BE A BLACKHEAD POPPER OR A PUS COLLECTOR AS YOUR FUTURE OCCUPATION?

142
WOULD YOU RATHER SPEND THE NIGHT IN A SWAMP WITH CROCODILES OR SPEND A NIGHT IN THE JUNGLE WITH A GORILLA?

143
WOULD YOU RATHER BE ATTACKED BY BATS OR BY AN ARMY OF SQUIRRELS?

144
WOULD YOU RATHER HAVE TO BURP EVERY TIME YOU BLINKED OR SING "THE HOKEY POKEY" EVERY TIME YOU OPENED YOUR MOUTH?

145
WOULD YOU RATHER HAVE 8 LEGS LIKE A SPIDER OR WINGS LIKE A MOTH?

146

WOULD YOU RATHER HAVE YOUR BIG TOE EATEN SLOWLY BY MAGGOTS OR HAVE IT BITTEN OFF BY A RABID DOG?

147

WOULD YOU RATHER LET A SNAKE SLITHER ALONG YOUR BODY OR BE TRAPPED IN AN ELEVATOR FOR 2 HOURS?

148

WOULD YOU RATHER FALL INTO A BARREL OF HONEY OR GET STUNG BY 10 BEES?

149

WOULD YOU RATHER SLEEP IN A CAVE FULL OF BATS OR SNAKES FOR ONE NIGHT?

150

WOULD YOU RATHER SNEEZE OUT PEANUTS AND EAT THEM OR HAVE EAR WAX THAT CONTINUALLY DRIPPED FROM YOUR EAR?

151

WOULD YOU RATHER DRINK SEAWEED WATER OR EAT BEEF TONGUE?

152

WOULD YOU RATHER WAKE UP WITH A SPIDER IN YOUR MOUTH OR BE TRAPPED IN A HUMAN-SIZED SPIDER WEB?

153

WOULD YOU RATHER WALK AROUND WITH POOPY TOILET PAPER STICKING OUT OF YOUR PANTS OR FORGET TO WEAR UNDERWEAR AND HAVE AN ACCIDENT?

154

WOULD YOU RATHER HAVE A TONGUE SO LONG IT DIDN'T FIT IN YOUR MOUTH OR HAVE EARS LIKE A WOLF?

155

WOULD YOU RATHER BE ATTACKED BY A MILLION LADYBUGS OR DIVED BOMBED OVER AND OVER BY A HAWK?

156
WOULD YOU RATHER HAVE AN EXPLOSIVE BOUT OF DIARRHEA OR HAVE A CAN OF GROUND UP WORMS EXPLODE IN YOUR CAR?

157
WOULD YOU RATHER HAVE THE ABILITY TO MOVE DOG POOP WITH YOUR BRAIN OR MAKE OTHER PEOPLE FART ON COMMAND?

158
WOULD YOU RATHER HAVE A THOUSAND BLACKHEADS ON YOUR FACE OR NOSE HAIR THAT KEPT GROWING NO MATTER WHAT?

159
WOULD YOU RATHER HAVE YOUR HEAD ON UPSIDE DOWN OR HAVE FEET ON YOUR HANDS?

160
WOULD YOU RATHER HAVE A TAIL LIKE A HORSE OR PAWS LIKE A CAT?

161
WOULD YOU RATHER HAVE SKIN LIKE COTTAGE CHEESE OR THE WRINKLES OF A 100 YEAR OLD?

162
WOULD YOU RATHER SWEAT NACHO CHEESE OR SMELL LIKE A DOG WHEN YOU SWEAT?

163
WOULD YOU RATHER HAVE A TAPEWORM LIVE IN YOUR STOMACH OR GET BIT BY A SNAKE?

164
WOULD YOU RATHER OPEN UP A RESTAURANT WITH FOOD MADE FROM VOMIT OR BE THROWN IN JAIL FOR 10 YEARS FOR A CRIME YOU DIDN'T COMMIT?

165
WOULD YOU RATHER MAKE A SOUND LIKE A DONKEY EVERY TIME YOU OPENED YOUR MOUTH OR HAVE A DUCK BILL?

166
WOULD YOU RATHER BE CHASED BY AN ANGRY BULL OR BY RATTLESNAKES?

167
WOULD YOU RATHER EAT A CORNDOG-FLAVORED POPSICLE OR A CHEESEBURGER-FLAVORED DONUT?

168
WOULD YOU RATHER SPRAY PHLEGM EVERY TIME YOU TALK OR FART EVERY TIME YOU SNEEZE?

169
WOULD YOU RATHER BE STUCK IN A REALLY SMALL BOX FOR 48 HOURS OR HAVE A TARANTULA CRAWL ON YOU FOR 5 HOURS?

170
WOULD YOU RATHER BE A DOG POOP SHOVELER OR A SCIENTIST WHO STUDIES SCAB SAMPLES?

171
WOULD YOU RATHER EAT YOUR OWN TOE JAM OR GET SNEEZED ON BY A PERSON WHO IS SICK?

172
WOULD YOU RATHER MAKE A SANDWICH OUT OF TOE JAM OR DRINK A GLASS OF PUS?

173
WOULD YOU RATHER EAT A BOWL OF HAIR OR GO BALD FOR THE REST OF YOUR LIFE?

174
WOULD YOU RATHER COLLECT ROTTEN TEETH OR TOENAIL CLIPPINGS?

175
WOULD YOU RATHER EAT A CAN OF DOG FOOD OR GO WITHOUT FOOD FOR FIVE DAYS?

176
WOULD YOU RATHER FIGHT AGAINST AN ARMY OF GIANT COCKROACHES OR ONE VENOMOUS SNAKE?

177
WOULD YOU RATHER HAVE WINGS LIKE A FLY OR ANTENNA LIKE A COCKROACH?

178
WOULD YOU RATHER LIVE TO BE 100 BUT BE IN EXCRUCIATING PAIN EVERY DAY OR DIE 5 YEARS FROM NOW?

179
WOULD YOU RATHER EAT A BOWL OF ICE CREAM WITH EARWIGS FOR SPRINKLES OR NEVER EAT YOUR FAVORITE FOOD EVER AGAIN?

180
WOULD YOU RATHER TAKE OUT THE GARBAGE ALL DAY OR SCRUB TOILETS ALL DAY?

181

WOULD YOU RATHER CLIMB UP A MOUNTAIN BEING CHASED BY WILD PIGS OR SWIM IN A POND BEING CHASED BY TEN EELS?

182

WOULD YOU RATHER HAVE TO WEAR DIAPERS OR DROOL CONSTANTLY FROM YOUR MOUTH?

183

WOULD YOU RATHER SMELL LIKE ROTTEN CHEESE OR HAVE SKIN THE TEXTURE OF ROTTEN FRUIT?

184

WOULD YOU RATHER PERMANENTLY LOSE AN EYEBALL OR ALL OF YOUR TEETH?

185

WOULD YOU RATHER BE ATTACKED BY PIRATES OR GET ATTACKED BY A SHARK?

186

WOULD YOU RATHER MAKE A SNOW ANGEL IN A PILE OF RAW FISH OR BUILD A SNOWMAN OUT OF RAW HAMBURGER MEAT?

187

WOULD YOU RATHER EAT A BOWL OF EAR WAX OR A BOWL OF EARWIGS?

188

WOULD YOU RATHER PLAY IN A BOUNCE HOUSE WITH A SNAKE OR GET CAUGHT UP IN THE DRAGLINES OF A GIANT SPIDER'S WEB?

189

WOULD YOU RATHER LOOK LIKE A BEAVER BUT HAVE LOTS OF FRIENDS OR BE THE MOST BEAUTIFUL PERSON IN THE WORLD AND HAVE NO FRIENDS?

190

WOULD YOU RATHER HAVE THE ABILITY TO SPIT OUT LAVA OR THE ABILITY TO FART OUT A RAINBOW?

191
WOULD YOU RATHER LOSE YOUR PHONE IN A BUCKET OF SCABS OR A BUCKET OF DOG POOP?

192
WOULD YOU RATHER EAT A TEASPOON OF GHOST PEPPER SPICE OR EAT A TABLESPOON OF SALT?

193
WOULD YOU RATHER BE STUCK ON THE TOP FLOOR OF A 60-STORY TOWER FOR TWO HOURS OR BE SMASHED IN THE CORNER OF A CROWDED ELEVATOR FOR TWO HOURS?

194
WOULD YOU RATHER HAVE A HEAD OF A COW OR A MOUTH OF A DONKEY?

195
WOULD YOU RATHER EAT A BOWL OF CRICKETS FOR DINNER OR DRINK A LARGE GLASS OF EXPIRED, CHUNKY MILK?

196
WOULD YOU RATHER EAT ROTTEN EGG JELLY OR YOGURT COVERED IN NOSE HAIRS?

197
WOULD YOU RATHER HAVE ONLY ONE TOOTH OR HAVE YOUR ENTIRE MOUTH FILLED WITH SHARP TALONS THAT MAKE IT DIFFICULT TO CLOSE YOUR MOUTH?

198
WOULD YOU RATHER BE CHASED BY A TEN FOOT CHICKEN OR ATTACKED BY AN ARMY OF BATS?

199
WOULD YOU RATHER FIGHT AN OSTRICH FOR TEN MINUTES OR BE CHASED BY A ZOMBIE FOR TWO MINUTES?

200
WOULD YOU RATHER BE ABLE TO BLOW SNOT BUBBLES OUT OF YOUR EARS OR SHOOT NOODLES OUT OF YOUR NOSE?

201

WOULD YOU RATHER HAVE ANTS IN YOUR PANTS OR DO THE BOOGIE DANCE IN FRONT OF 2,000 PEOPLE?

202

WOULD YOU RATHER HAVE AN ITCHY EAR OR AN ITCHY BUTT FOR THE REST OF YOUR LIFE?

203

WOULD YOU RATHER HAVE TO USE CHAPSTICK THAT SMELLS AND TASTES LIKE KETCHUP OR DEODORANT THAT SMELLS LIKE MUSTARD?

204

WOULD YOU RATHER GO A WEEK WITHOUT TOILET PAPER OR A WEEK WITHOUT A WAY TO SHOWER OR WASH DISHES?

205

WOULD YOU RATHER HAVE HEAD LICE OR HAVE A SPIDER THAT CRAWLS ON YOU EVERY NIGHT BUT YOU DON'T EVEN KNOW IT?

206

WOULD YOU RATHER GET TRAMPLED BY A STAMPEDE OF PEOPLE AT A CONCERT AND END UP IN A HOSPITAL IN SERIOUS CONDITION OR BE GORED BY A BULL AND SURVIVE?

207

WOULD YOU RATHER HAVE A CENTIPEDE CRAWL INTO YOUR MOUTH OR HAVE A WORM MAKE A HOME IN YOUR EAR?

208

WOULD YOU RATHER HAVE A TAIL LIKE A COW OR A HEAD LIKE A GOAT?

209

WOULD YOU RATHER HAVE TALONS LIKE AN EAGLE OR WALK EVERYWHERE LIKE A CRAB?

210

WOULD YOU RATHER HAVE A PET THAT BIT EVERYONE IT CAME INTO CONTACT WITH OR GOT BIT BY EVERY ANIMAL YOU PETTED?

211

WOULD YOU RATHER SOMEONE BLOW HOT BREATH IN YOUR EAR OR FART NEAR YOUR NOSE?

212

WOULD YOU RATHER PICK SOMEONE'S BOOGERS OUT OF THEIR NOSE OR POP THE ZITS ON THEIR BACK?

213

WOULD YOU RATHER HAVE TO BRING YOUR OWN TOILET WITH YOU EVERYWHERE YOU WENT OR BE STUCK IN A CROWDED BUS AND HAVE AN EXPLOSIVE POOP ACCIDENT?

214

WOULD YOU RATHER CHEW GUM THAT TASTES LIKE LIVER OR HAVE BREATH THAT SMELLS LIKE DOG POOP?

215

WOULD YOU RATHER WEAR PANTS MADE WITH STINGING NETTLES OR HAVE TO WEAR INVISIBLE CLOTHES?

216

WOULD YOU RATHER BE AN EYE BOOGER COLLECTOR OR TOE JAM COLLECTOR?

217

WOULD YOU RATHER SHAVE YOUR HEAD OR HAVE DANDRUFF SO BADLY THAT YOU LEAVE WHITE DUST WHEREVER YOU GO?

218

WOULD YOU RATHER EAT FOOD OUT OF A GARBAGE CAN OR URINATE IN PUBLIC?

219

WOULD YOU RATHER FART OUT OF YOUR MOUTH OR SNEEZE OUT OF YOUR BUTT?

220

WOULD YOU RATHER HAVE FINGERS THAT LOOK LIKE PICKLES OR A HEAD THE SIZE OF A GRAPEFRUIT?

221

WOULD YOU RATHER LOSE YOUR TEETH BECAUSE THEY ROTTED AWAY OR HAVE SUPER LARGE RABBIT TEETH?

222

WOULD YOU RATHER BE TRAPPED IN A ROOM WITH A SKUNK OR BE DIVE BOMBED BY A FLOCK OF CROWS?

223

WOULD YOU RATHER HAVE A CLOWN FACE OR A BODY OF A TROLL?

224

WOULD YOU RATHER SPEND A YEAR STRANDED BY YOURSELF ON A DESERT ISLAND OR TRAPPED TEN YEARS BY YOURSELF IN AN AMUSEMENT PARK?

225

WOULD YOU RATHER HAVE YOUR UNDERWEAR ALWAYS BE WET OR HAVE TO SLEEP IN A WET BED EVERY NIGHT?

226
WOULD YOU RATHER HAVE TO THROW UP IN AN
OUTHOUSE OR HAVE A DOG PEE ON YOU?

227
WOULD YOU RATHER EAT A JAR OF PICKLED PIGS FEET
OR EAT SHEEP BRAIN?

228
WOULD YOU RATHER BE IN A POOL OF MAPLE SYRUP
FOR TWO HOURS WITH A SWARM OF MOSQUITOES
WAITING FOR YOU OR FIND YOURSELF IN A BEE COLONY
AND BE MISTAKEN FOR THE QUEEN BEE?

229
WOULD YOU RATHER HAVE FEET LIKE A MONKEY OR FEET
LIKE A CHICKEN?

230
WOULD YOU RATHER HAVE THE CREEPY FEELING THAT
SOMEONE IS FOLLOWING YOU EVERY DAY FOR THE REST
OF YOUR LIFE OR BE CHASED BY A CLOWN ONCE
A WEEK?

231

WOULD YOU RATHER SWEAT STICKY GLUE OR HAVE FARTS THAT TURN INTO WRITHING SNAKES?

232

WOULD YOU RATHER NOT BE ABLE TO TELL THE DIFFERENCE BETWEEN A DOG AND A DONUT OR WAKE UP EVERY DAY AND FORGET WHO YOUR FAMILY IS?

233

WOULD YOU RATHER JOIN YOUR BEST FRIEND IN A BATTLE AGAINST ZOMBIES OR RUN AWAY TO SOMEPLACE SAFE?

234

WOULD YOU RATHER GET A TOOTHPICK SHOVED UNDERNEATH ALL YOUR TOENAILS OR WALK DOWN A STREET OF BROKEN GLASS WITH BARE FEET?

235

WOULD YOU RATHER EAT A DIRTY BAND-AID OR STUB YOUR TOE SO HARD YOU HAVE TO REMOVE THE NAIL?

236
WOULD YOU RATHER WORK ALL DAY AT A PIG FARM OR WASH YOUR HANDS WITH UNFLUSHED TOILET WATER?

237
WOULD YOU RATHER HAVE THE ABILITY TO TRANSFORM INTO A MEMBER OF THE OPPOSIT SEX OR AS A CENTIPEDE WITH SUPER POWERS?

238
WOULD YOU RATHER EAT THE FOOD CAUGHT IN A STRANGE MAN'S BEARD OR EAT YOUR OWN EARWAX?

239
WOULD YOU RATHER EAT WORMS TO TEMPORARILY GAIN SUPER SPEED OR EAT CRUNCHY COCKROACHES TO TEMPORARILY GAIN SUPER STRENGTH?

240
WOULD YOU RATHER SHAVE YOUR EYEBROWS OR HAVE A BUSHY UNIBROW?

241

WOULD YOU RATHER GET THROWN OFF A 30-FOOT BRIDGE OR GET WATERBOARDED?

242

WOULD YOU RATHER DISCOVER HALF A WORM INSIDE AN APPLE OR FIND A DEAD COCKROACH IN YOUR SANDWICH?

243

WOULD YOU RATHER EAT RAW CHICKEN OR HAVE TO PLUCK THE FEATHERS OFF A LIVE CHICKEN?

244

WOULD YOU RATHER HAVE YOUR HEAD SHAPED LIKE AN APPLE OR YOUR BODY SHAPED LIKE AN APPLE?

245

WOULD YOU RATHER HAVE BIG EYES LIKE A CARTOON CHARACTER OR FOUR FINGERS LIKE A CARTOON CHARACTER?

246
WOULD YOU RATHER GET CHASED BY A GIANT CORN DOG OR STUCK INSIDE A COTTON CANDY MACHINE?

247
WOULD YOU RATHER BE GIVEN A WEDGIE AND THEN HUNG UP BY YOUR UNDERWEAR ON A BRIDGE OR BE GIVEN A SWIRLY EVERY DAY FOR A WEEK?

248
WOULD YOU RATHER HAVE PEANUT BUTTER NACHOS FOR LUNCH OR WAFFLES WITH HOT SAUCE FOR BREAKFAST?

249
WOULD YOU RATHER EAT A STICK OF DEODORANT OR SMELL REALLY BADLY OF B.O. FOR THE REST OF YOUR LIFE?

250
WOULD YOU RATHER PLAY IN THE SNOW WEARING FLIP FLOPS OR PLAY IN THE DESERT DRESSED FOR A BLIZZARD?

251
WOULD YOU RATHER STICK YOUR TONGUE ON A FREEZING POLE OR SIT INSIDE OF A WALK-IN FRIDGE FOR AN HOUR?

252
WOULD YOU RATHER BE STUCK IN A HAUNTED HOUSE BY YOURSELF OR HAVE YOUR BEST FRIEND TURN INTO A ZOMBIE?

253
WOULD YOU RATHER BE CHASED BY A ZOMBIE OR A GIANT RABID SQUIRREL?

254
WOULD YOU RATHER HAVE GUM STUCK BETWEEN YOUR TOES OR MELTED CHEESE BETWEEN YOUR ARMPITS?

255
WOULD YOU RATHER GET STUCK IN A ROCK SLIDE OR AN AVALANCHE?

256
WOULD YOU RATHER WALK AROUND IN A POOPY DIAPER OR TALK LIKE A BABY FOR A WHOLE DAY?

257
WOULD YOU RATHER NOT KNOW THE DIFFERENCE BETWEEN YOUR BEST FRIEND AND A COOKIE OR NOT KNOW THE DIFFERENCE BETWEEN DOG POO AND A BROWNIE?

258
WOULD YOU RATHER HAVE THE BODY OF A HIPPO OR A HEAD OF A SPIDER?

259
WOULD YOU RATHER HAVE YOUR WORST NIGHTMARE ON REPEAT EVERYTIME YOU GO TO BED OR NEVER BE ABLE TO SLEEP AGAIN?

260
WOULD YOU RATHER TAKE A NAP IN A TUB FULL OF WORMS OR ROLL AROUND IN FRESH COW MANURE?

261

WOULD YOU RATHER HAVE 100 SPLINTERS ON THE BOTTOM OF YOUR FEET OR 100 CANKER SORES IN YOUR MOUTH?

262

WOULD YOU RATHER BE STUCK IN YOUR ROOM FOR A MONTH WITHOUT SEEING YOUR FRIENDS OR DRINK A GIANT GLASS OF LAXATIVES RIGHT BEFORE GOING OUT WITH YOUR FRIENDS?

263

WOULD YOU RATHER HAVE YOUR FRIENDS SNEEZE SNOT ONTO YOUR FACE OR BLOW THEIR NOSE USING YOUR SHIRT SLEEVE?

264

WOULD YOU RATHER DRINK YOUR FAVORITE BEVERAGE WITH MAYONNAISE ICE CUBES OR DRINK A PITCHER OF PICKLE JUICE?

265
WOULD YOU RATHER TRY TO CONVINCE PEOPLE THAT YOU ARE VISITING FROM THE FUTURE AND GOT HERE BY TIME TRAVEL OR THAT YOU ARE AN ALIEN AND YOUR NAME IS SPORK?

266
WOULD YOU RATHER LOOK LIKE A HOT DOG OR HAVE BLEAT LIKE A GOAT EVERY TIME YOU TRY TO TALK?

267
WOULD YOU RATHER USE TOOTHPASTE AS LOTION OR MAYONNAISE AS MOUTHWASH?

268
WOULD YOU RATHER TURN TINY AND LIVE IN SOMEONE ELSE'S NOSE FOR 24 HOURS OR TURN INTO A GIANT FOR 24 HOURS AND NOT HAVE ANY CLOTHES TO COVER UP WITH?

269
WOULD YOU RATHER EAT POPCORN PICKED UP OFF THE MOVIE THEATER FLOOR OR DRINK A HALF-FINISHED COFFEE YOU FOUND ON TOP OF THE GARBAGE CAN LID?

270
WOULD YOU RATHER SLEEP IN A TRUCK STOP
BATHROOM OR COOK DINNER AT THE CITY DUMP?

271
WOULD YOU RATHER LAUGH WHENEVER SOMEONE SAYS
SOMETHING SAD OR CRY WHENEVER SOMEONE SAYS
SOMETHING FUNNY?

272
WOULD YOU RATHER WIN A MILLION DOLLARS AND CUT
OFF YOUR BIG TOE OR BE A 100,000 IN DEBT?

273
WOULD YOU RATHER HAVE SILENT BUT SUPER SMELLY
FARTS OR SUPER LOUD FARTS THAT DON'T SMELL
AT ALL?

274
WOULD YOU RATHER BE TRAPPED IN YOUR FAVORITE
MOVIE OR BE TRAPPED IN YOUR FAVORITE VIDEO GAME?

275
WOULD YOU RATHER HAVE A BOOGER THAT IS CONSTANTLY STICKING OUT OF YOUR NOSE OR A BIG PIECE OF SHREDDED MEAT ALWAYS STUCK BETWEEN YOUR TEETH?

276
WOULD YOU RATHER EAT A CIGARETTE BUTT OR PULL A SCAB OFF OF A STRANGER?

277
WOULD YOU RATHER BE FORCED TO ROB A BANK AND HAVE TO LIVE THE REST OF YOUR LIFE ON THE RUN OR BE BLAMED FOR A CRIME YOU DIDN'T COMMIT AND HAVE TO GO TO JAIL FOR 1 YEAR?

278
WOULD YOU RATHER BE BURIED UP TO YOUR NECK IN SAND AND THEN LEFT BY YOUR FRIENDS OR BE CHASED AND BIT BY HUNDREDS OF SAND FLEAS?

279
WOULD YOU RATHER BE IN AN OUTHOUSE WHEN IT IS TIPPED OVER OR BE CHASED BY A POOP MONSTER?

280
WOULD YOU RATHER TURN NEON YELLOW EVERY TIME YOU ARE EMBARRASSED OR HAVE TO WALK AROUND LIKE A CRAB TO GET TO WHERE YOU ARE GOING?

281
WOULD YOU RATHER BARK LIKE A DOG EVERY TIME SOMEONE SAID YOUR NAME OR NOT BE ABLE TO TALK AT ALL?

282
WOULD YOU RATHER GURINATE IN PUBLIC OR USE A SNAKE FOR A JUMP ROPE?

283
WOULD YOU RATHER EAT ONLY CANDY OR ONLY PIZZA FOR A YEAR?

284
WOULD YOU RATHER EAT A WHOLE STICK OF BUTTER OR A CUP OF MAYONNAISE?

285
WOULD YOU RATHER BE A GENIUS AND LOOK LIKE A CLOWN OR BE REALLY DUMB BUT DROP-DEAD GORGEOUS?

286
WOULD YOU RATHER GET INTO A ZOMBIE FIGHT OR GET ATTACKED BY A SHARK?

287
WOULD YOU RATHER HAVE A BUNCH OF FRIENDS THAT ARE NOT REALLY YOUR FRIENDS OR ONE TRUE FRIEND THAT IS A SQUIRREL?

288
WOULD YOU RATHER HAVE YOUR SNOWMAN COME TO LIFE OR HAVE SANTA BE REAL?

289

WOULD YOU RATHER BE FORCED TO EAT YOUR FAVORITE FOOD FOR 24 HOURS UNTIL YOU GET SICK OR NOT EVER EAT YOUR FAVORITE FOOD AGAIN?

290

WOULD YOU RATHER GET SPRAYED IN THE FACE BY A SKUNK OR BIT BY A SHARK?

291

WOULD YOU RATHER LOSE YOUR SENSE OF SMELL OR YOUR SENSE OF TOUCH?

292

WOULD YOU RATHER EAT A LIVE SQUID OR A DEAD RAT?

293

WOULD YOU RATHER HAVE LEGS LIKE A FROG OR OCTOPUS ARMS?

294
WOULD YOU RATHER YOUR HOUSE BE INFESTED WITH MICE OR WITH SNAKES?

295
WOULD YOU RATHER COUGH UP A FUR BALL EVER TIME SOMEONE SAID HELLO OR PEE YOURSELF EVERY TIME YOU LAUGHED?

296
WOULD YOU RATHER SHED YOUR SKIN ONCE A WEEK LIKE A SNAKE OR CONSTANTLY TURN COLORS TO MATCH YOUR SURROUNDINGS LIKE A LIZARD?

297
WOULD YOU RATHER HAVE THE ABILITY TO WHISTLE THROUGH YOUR NOSE OR BURP UP PERFUME?

298
WOULD YOU RATHER HAVE A NOSE ON THE BOTTOM OF YOUR FOOT OR HAVE A MOUTH ON THE PALM OF YOUR HAND THAT TALKED ON ITS OWN?

299

WOULD YOU RATHER HAVE HOOVES LIKE A HORSE OR CHEW CUD LIKE A COW?

300

WOULD YOU RATHER YOUR FEET BE SO STINKY THAT NO ONE COULD TOLERATE BEING NEAR YOU OR BE ABLE TO SMELL EVERYONE'S FEET ALL THE TIME?

301

WOULD YOU RATHER HAVE RANCID BREATH OR FART EXCESSIVELY?

302

WOULD YOU RATHER HAVE EARS THAT KEPT GROWING FOR THE REST OF YOUR LIFE OR TEETH?

303

WOULD YOU RATHER SWIM IN A POOL OF DOG DROOL OR MUSTARD?

304
WOULD YOU RATHER WEAR THE SAME PAIR OF UNDERWEAR FOR A YEAR, OR NOT WEAR ANY UNDERWEAR FOR A YEAR?

305
WOULD YOU RATHER EAT A LIVE TARANTULA OR DRINK A WORM MILKSHAKE?

306
WOULD YOU RATHER EAT A PEE SLUSHY OR FRIES DIPPED IN GOOSE POOP SAUCE?

307
WOULD YOU RATHER HAVE TO GARNISH ALL YOUR FOOD WITH MAGGOTS OR HAVE TO DRINK A SLUG SMOOTHIE AFTER EVERY MEAL?

308
WOULD YOU RATHER BE EATEN ALIVE BY MOSQUITOES OR JUMP INTO AN ALLIGATOR TANK?

309
WOULD YOU RATHER EAT SLUG SUSHI OR TOENAIL PUDDING?

310
WOULD YOU RATHER HAVE TO WALK AROUND WITH TUNA FISH IN YOUR SOCKS OR CANNED DOG FOOD IN YOUR PANTS?

311
WOULD YOU RATHER BE LOCKED IN A ROOM THREE FEET DEEP WITH TUNA FISH FOR A YEAR OR LOCKED IN A ROOM WITH A MILLION TICKS FOR A WEEK?

312
WOULD YOU RATHER EAT A BOWL OF FINGERNAILS OR EAT A GROUNDED HORSE HOOF?

313
WOULD YOU RATHER LIVE IN THE SEWER OR A DOG FOOD CANNING FACILITY?

314
WOULD YOU RATHER EAT SPOILED FOOD FOR THE REST OF YOUR LIFE OR CANNED CAT FOOD?

315
WOULD YOU RATHER LIVE IN A DIRTY PORT-A-POT OR WOULD YOU RATHER EAT MAGGOT-INFESTED RABBIT CARCASS?

316
WOULD YOU RATHER SWIM IN A PEE POOL WITH A CROWD OR GET POOPED ON BY A FLOCK OF INTESTINALLY-CHALLENGED PELICANS?

317
WOULD YOU RATHER PEE IN THE POOL WHILE SWIMMING WITH YOUR BEST-FRIENDS - TURNING THE WATER GREEN - OR ACCIDENTALLY WALK IN FRONT OF YOUR FRIENDS WITHOUT ANY OF YOUR CLOTHES ON?

318

WOULD YOU RATHER VOMIT UNCONTROLLABLY FOR THE REST OF THE DAY EVERY TIME YOU SEE A BIRD OR HAVE SNOT POOR OUT OF YOU NOSE EVERY TIME YOU HEAR A VOICE?

319

WOULD YOU RATHER BE STUCK IN A CUBE OF JELLO FOR 24 HOURS OR BE FORCED TO EAT 20 PLATES OF JELLO IN ONE DAY?

320

WOULD YOU RATHER TIGHTROPE WALK ONE MILE OVER A HUGE ALLIGATOR TANK OR HAVE TO SWIM IN A POND FULL OF SHARKS?

321

WOULD YOU RATHER BE STUCK IN A TREE SURROUNDED BY A WOLF PACK OR BE TRAPPED -AND ALMOST SUFFOCATING- UNDER A WHOLE PIT OF SWEET KITTENS?

322

WOULD YOU RATHER HAVE A GARDEN GROWING ON THE TOP OF YOUR HEAD OR MOSS GROWING ON YOUR ARMS?

323

WOULD YOU RATHER HAVE A RABID ATTACK RAT AS A BODYGUARD OR A 50 VENOMOUS SNAILS?

324

WOULD YOU RATHER CARTWHEEL ON A SLACKLINE SUSPENDED OVER A SWAMP WITH ALLIGATORS OR JUMP OUT OF AN AIRPLANE -WITH A PARACHUTE- OVER THE OCEAN?

325

WOULD YOU RATHER HAVE TO TRY TO HOLD OPEN AN ALLIGATOR'S MOUTH FOR A WHOLE HOUR OR TRY TO RIDE AN ANGRY BULL FOR ONE HOUR?

326

WOULD YOU RATHER SWIM ACROSS THE PACIFIC OCEAN OR RUN ACROSS AFRICA?

327

WOULD YOU RATHER HAVE TO DO 100 PULL-UPS ON A BAR SUSPENDED ABOVE ROCKY GROUND OR HAVE TO DO 150 PUSH-UPS OVER A GAP BETWEEN TWO CLIFFS?

328

WOULD YOU RATHER ALL OF THE CONDIMENTS IN YOUR FRIDGE COME ALIVE, OR ALL THE VEGETABLES IN YOUR KITCHEN?

329

WOULD YOU RATHER HAVE THE HIC-UPS FOR THE REST OF YOUR LIFE OR ALWAYS FEEL LIKE YOUR GOING TO SNEEZE BUT CAN'T?

330

WOULD YOU RATHER BEAT A VENGEFUL PIRATE IN POKER OR WALK THE PLANK?

331

WOULD YOU RATHER BE FORCED TO ONLY HAVE TWO HOURS OF SLEEP A NIGHT OR HAVE TO SLEEP 23 HOURS IN A DAY?

332

WOULD YOU RATHER BE ONE CENTIMETER TALL OR BE 25 FEET TALL?

333

WOULD YOU RATHER BE AN EGYPTION MUMMY STUCK IN THE PRESENT OR A MODERN DAY PERSON STUCK IN ANCIENT EGYPTION TIMES?

334

WOULD YOU RATHER SWIM IN WATER FILLED WITH PIRANHAS OR WADE WAIST DEEP IN WATER WITH ONE SHARK?

335

WOULD YOU RATHER YOUR SHOES HAVE WINGS SO YOU CAN FLOW A COUPLE FEET OFF THE GROUND OR A HAT WITH A PROPELLER SO YOU CAN HOVER CLOSE TO THE GROUND?

336

WOULD YOU RATHER YOUR SHOES HAD A MIND OF THEIR OWN AND WALKED WHEREVER THEY WANTED OR YOUR HAT SENDS THOUGHTS INTO YOUR HEAD THAT AREN'T YOURS?

337

WOULD YOU RATHER BE BITTEN BY A WEREWOLF OR A VAMPIRE?

338

WOULD YOU RATHER AN EVIL OCTOPUS BECAME DICTATOR OR HAVE A CLINGY STARFISH BE YOUR MOM?

339

WOULD YOU RATHER HAVE TO RUN ACROSS THE WHOLE GREAT WALL OF CHINA WITH WOLVES CHASING YOU OR BE BOUND TO A BALL AND CHAIN WHILE FIGHTING TO THE DEATH AGAINST A SAMURAI?

340
WOULD YOU RATHER DRIVE YOUR CAR THROUGH LAVA OR BE DOG-PILED BY CANNIBALISTIC ZOMBIES?

341
WOULD YOU RATHER HAVE TO SWIM ACROSS THE ATLANTIC OCEAN OR RUN THE ENTIRE GREAT WALL OF CHINA?

342
WOULD YOU RATHER HAVE NO FACIAL FEATURES EXCEPT YOUR EYES OR HAVE A NOSE AND A MOUTH BUT NO EYES?

343
WOULD YOU RATHER HAVE EXCESSIVELY LONG EAR HAIRS OR LONG NOSTRIL HAIRS?

344
WOULD YOU RATHER WORK AS A SECRET AGENT FOR THE BAD GUYS OR WORK AS A JANITOR FOR THE GOOD GUYS?

345

WOULD YOU RATHER HAVE TO DRINK DIRTY TOILET WATER OR GET SPRAYED BY A SKUNK?

346

WOULD YOU RATHER GO OFF NIAGARA FALLS IN A CANOE OR JUMP OUT OF AN AIRPLANE IN A VERY OLD PARACHUTE?

347

WOULD YOU RATHER YOUR SIZE CHANGED EVERY DAY, OR YOUR APPEARANCE?

348

WOULD YOU RATHER BE FORCED TO PLEDGE UNDYING LOYALTY TO A WEASEL OR BECOME ENSLAVED BY A TERRIBLE SORCEROUS?

349

WOULD YOU RATHER ONLY DRINK WATER FOR THE REST OF YOUR LIFE OR NEVER EAT ANOTHER BITE OF DESSERT?

BONUS QUESTIONS!

FROM THE FIRST EDITION
NOW AVAILABLE ON AMAZON!

DO YOU HAVE WHAT IT TAKES? CAN YOU ANSWER
THESE THOUGH-PROVOKING WOULD YOU
RATHER QUESTIONS?!

350
WOULD YOU RATHER TRIP EVERY TIME YOU LOOKED
LEFT, OR SNEEZE EVERY TIME YOU USED YOUR RIGHT
HAND?

351
WOULD YOU RATHER HAVE FIVE OF YOUR TEETH PULLED OR HAVE TO BE BEST FRIENDS WITH YOUR LEAST FAVORITE PERSON?

352
WOULD YOU RATHER HAVE A NECK TWO FEET LONG OR HAVE EARS LIKE AN ELEPHANT?

353
WOULD YOU RATHER BE 7 FEET TALL AND REALLY WEAK, OR 3 FEET TALL AND STRONG AS AN OX?

354
WOULD YOU RATHER LOSE YOUR SIGHT AND SMELL OR YOUR HEARING AND TASTE?

355
WOULD YOU RATHER HAVE EYES SO BIG YOU LOOKED LIKE A CARTOON CHARACTER OR SPEECH BUBBLES THAT POPPED UP EVERY TIME YOU SAID ANYTHING?

356
WOULD YOU RATHER HAVE TO SING EVERYTHING YOU SAID OUT LOUD OR BE MUTE?

357
WOULD YOU RATHER HAVE TO CRAWL AROUND ON ALL FOURS FOR THE REST OF YOUR LIFE OR HAVE A TAIL LIKE A FOX?

358
WOULD YOU RATHER BE THE BEST ATHLETE IN THE WORLD BUT NOT VERY SMART, OR BE THE SMARTEST PERSON IN THE WORLD BUT BE CRIPPLED IN A WHEELCHAIR?

359
WOULD YOU RATHER NEVER BE ABLE TO STOP READING OR NOT KNOW HOW TO READ?

360
WOULD YOU RATHER BE A JANITOR BUT MAKE $100,000 A YEAR OR HAVE YOUR DREAM JOB AND MAKE $20,000 A YEAR?

Printed in Great Britain
by Amazon